Introduction

Transfer paints are so underused and undervalued that we thought it was time to redress the balance and give them a fair hearing. So often we hear people groan at the mention of the words. They say they have tried them in the past but the results were unsatisfactory or the colours garish and unpredictable.

In this book we aim to shatter some of the negative attitudes towards these underrated fabric paints by exploring strategies for developing colour sensitivity as well as awareness of fabric and surface qualities which may be enriched by transfer colouring in any of its many forms. As with other potentially exciting techniques the secret lies in working at it through a series of experimental samples to discover the huge possibilities.

This is the opportunity to use your ironing skills in a really creative way. It is possible to layer, overprint and build up to rich and complex surfaces as well as create delicate and atmospheric imagery.

Transfer printing can appear softly textured and subtly coloured as well as bold and vibrant. Unlike other methods it can be printed as a hard edged design or as 'in and out' of focus images along with tints, washes and an amazing array of decorative marks all without spoiling the surface feel of the fabric. These unique characteristics can feature in your work or be used just as a means of transferring the design in colour to the fabric.

With practise it is possible to achieve predictable results but there are times when some wonderfully surprising effects, when combining images, can trigger good ideas for designs to be carried out in a range of techniques.

All that we would ask is that you don't finally give up on transfer paints until you have explored some of the ideas in this book, because given the opportunity we can't believe that you won't want to keep using them as a valuable tool in your design and technique vocabulary.

What are Transfer Paints?

Transfer paints are a liquid or crayon colouring medium which are applied to paper and then ironed off onto fabric to produce a coloured image.

They can be bought ready mixed into a liquid which may be watered down for more delicate colours although they then become more difficult to use for mono printing etc.. It is usually possible to buy a colourless thickener to lighten the colour whilst retaining a thick enough consistency for printing purposes.

They are produced in powder form and called disperse dyes. These come in a range of colours and can be mixed to form even

more colours. Although they are usually thinner when mixed there is a thickener available to add to them so that they can be used for printing and mono printing.

Fabric transfer crayons are readily available and many people find them coarse and garish but once again they can be rewarding if time is spent to work on the sensitive use of applying and mixing the colours. Transfer fabric pens with fibre tips can be suitable for some projects but they are not so easy to find.

One very useful aspect of these dyes is that several prints may be ironed off from each piece of paper depending on the

thickness of the paint and the type of fabric. The exception to this is usually the crayons or a thin wash of paint from which is it normally only possible to make one successful print.

Inside cover: Hearts

This large cushion panel shows how easily transfer paints can be used in conjunction with other fabrics including recycled household materials to form pieced and patched cloths for practical or wall hung pieces. J.L.

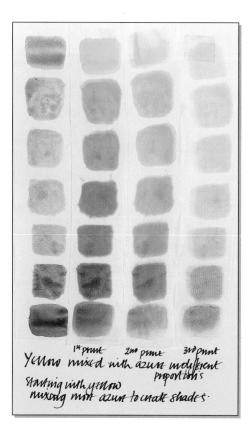

Above: Colour Mixing Notebook page. J.L.

Below: The basic equipment for transfer painting can be quite simple although the results produced look very professional. The mixing palette is standing on a much used printing mat (a metalised ironing sheet). It is possible to use a variety of brushes and sponges to apply the paint and the printing materials range from bought stencils and templates through plastic doilies, self-made stencils, printing blocks and plant cuttings. There are some interesting printing foams available which when heated can be imprinted with patterns and marks. This can be particularly useful when wanting a combination of positive and negative patterns.

Which is the best paper to use?

A non-absorbent thin PHOTOCOPYING or TYPING PAPER is perfectly adequate for these dyes as too thick a paper will prevent the heat from penetrating to make a good print. PATTERN CUTTING PAPER is also very good and the dyes should be painted on the shiny side. LAYOUT PAPER works well and has many advantages. It can be bought in several sizes, including A1 (840x594mm) and it is semi-transparent so particularly useful when dealing with the problem of reverse imagery. If you take an image which needs to be ironed off the right way round first draw it onto the layout pad as you wish it to be using a black fibre tip pen. Next turn the paper over and the image will be reversed and can be seen clearly through the paper. Colour the reverse image with the transfer paints and when dry turn it over and iron off where the image will transfer the correct way round. This could be relevant when using lettering.

The paper bag myth! We often hear how well paper bags will print off and in some cases this is true. The bags which do print off are those made from the paper which has been used in the manufacture of transfer printed fabrics. Huge quantities are used to print off the fabrics and once they have been used they are often recycled into craft bags or paper to wrap flowers (usually in markets). They can be used to print because they still have some transfer paint on them. If you feel the bags you will see

that they have one slightly shiny side and a coarser side which is quite characteristic. Depending on the colour and pattern, prints may be obtained. Bags other than this do not print off.

Types of Fabric

These transfer paints are designed to be used with synthetic or partially synthetic fabrics. They react to the heat and print onto the fabric. The higher the synthetic content the stronger and more permanent the colour. Types of fabric include closely woven, novelty, metallic and sheers. Many are cheap to buy although you can find beautiful polyester viscose fabrics which are more expensive but entirely appropriate if a hand quilted cushion design or other special project was envisaged.

SYNTHETIC VELVETS can be fabulous when transfer printed but they take a great deal of paint and leave little left for a second print. POLYCOTTON comes in various proportions and the more synthetic the stronger the colour. On polycotton with a high cotton content the colours may be more muted and many people prefer this. Cream, white or light colours are best for printing as the colours are clearer but other shades are possible if you bear in mind that there will be a colour distortion.

Most fabrics when bought have a 'dressing' which is a paste or starch which gives them a crisp effect. If transfer paints are applied to an unwashed fabric with such a surface, then some

of the image would be released with the 'paste' when washed. It is therefore best to use pre-washed fabrics (particularly polycotton). The backs of old plain COLOURED COTTON AND POLYESTER SHIRTS, SHEETS AND NET CURTAINS are all excellent to practice on.

Unless an uneven crumpled image is required always iron the fabrics before transferring the design. A slightly warm cloth seems to respond well and helps the printing off process. There are dynamic possibilities for exciting printed surfaces if a pieced fabric using a COMBINATION OF SYNTHETIC FIBRES AND LACES is used in place of a one piece background. The colours will react slightly differently on each fibre and the results could prove inspiring.

Colour Mixing

It is true that some garish colour combinations can occur when using transfer paints but it is possible to control the colour with practise. We have always advised notebooks for ongoing reference when experimenting with new media and this pays off particularly well with transfer paints.

There are many ways of achieving good results but a simple suggestion is to take two colours such as yellow and azure and to mix them with each other in various proportions to see how many different shades can be achieved. Small blocks of colour painted in this way in shade charts may not sound the most exciting way of using

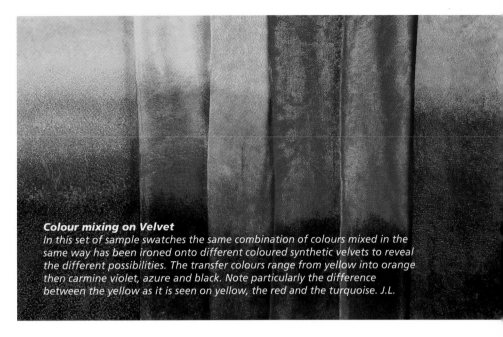

Colour mixing on Velvet
In this set of sample swatches the same combination of colours mixed in the same way has been ironed onto different coloured synthetic velvets to reveal the different possibilities. The transfer colours range from yellow into orange then carmine violet, azure and black. Note particularly the difference between the yellow as it is seen on yellow, the red and the turquoise. J.L.

transfer paints but it certainly pays dividends with written notes on the results. This can be carried out with numerous colour combinations but once you have done some it will make the exciting colouring possibilities mentioned in the book a lot more achievable.

• Iron off these little colour blocks onto a variety of synthetics to see the different reactions.

• Remember always to start with the LIGHTEST colour and add in the darker a little at a time and this will save you wasting a lot of time and colour by mixing light into dark.

• Yellow is an amazingly versatile colour which adds sparkle when mixed with the others in varying proportions, which means it is often used up first, so another hint is to buy at least two yellows to one of every other colour. Often yellow sells

out first so many people have learned this useful tip.

• Remember that when the colour is applied undiluted then the print will be very strong but it can be watered down to the extent that it may only look like coloured water and yet it will still print.

• Never waste any and rather than wash it out of the palette use up every drop to colour papers until you need them or make 'palette prints'.

• Although improved in recent years, transfer colours often appear darker on the paper and brighter on the fabric. Blues, greens, black and purple may be hard to distinguish on the mixing plate. Remember to mark or place the bottle adjacent to the palette. Alternatively not knowing or losing track of the colours can produce surprising colour schemes.

Applying the Paint

Almost any way in which colour may be applied can be utilised in the application of colour, pattern and texture to paper which is then transferred onto fabric.

• Although using a PAINTBRUSH is possible the results, if not carefully used, might look rigid. However the brushes with flattened ends or splayed out bristles make wonderful printed textures.

• SPONGES of all shapes and sizes are fantastic. They can have holes, be smooth or irregular and produce a huge array of textures. A little water on the sponge before adding the colour will often produce a marvellous stippled effect. Smooth sponges may be cut into shapes to make flexible printing blocks.

• JAY CLOTHS, DISH CLOTHS AND CRUMPLED PAPER TOWELS can be used to simulate the 'ragging' effects so popular in interior design.

• Fabric paints can be stippled onto the paper with a STIPPLING BRUSH or sprayed through a DIFFUSER or a make-up mist sprayer available at chemists. (Plant demisters require too much liquid to make them useful.)

• A PALETTE KNIFE can apply the paints in bold rhythmic swathes of colour and scrape at the surface to achieve marvellous rocks and organic structures.

• CARD 'COMBS' can drag patterns throughout a design.

• A very pale wash, almost water dirtied by a little transfer paint, is effective although it usually gives only one successful print.

• It is even possible to add washing up liquid and water and blow bubbles through a straw to achieve bubble prints.

• Paint applied thickly onto the paper will give several prints with varying results. The second one will often expose the textural qualities echoing the actual method of application such as brush or sponge.

• With a particular image that you wish to repeat it may be painted again on the same paper once the first print has been ironed off.

Ironing Off

We think that this is the main problem area of the whole procedure and that the reason why people have had so many 'failures' is that the ironing off has not been carried out with the following very important points in mind.

• THE IRON MUST BE HOT ENOUGH (even if it has just been switched off that few seconds can be crucial). Some irons for some reason do not get hot enough for a really successful print and travel irons often cannot be used in this way. Although not essential, flat irons are better than steam irons as the holes can cause irregular heat transfer and show on the finished print. Irons have hotter and cooler spots so for a really successful print it is better to gently move the iron over the whole area without moving the paper. In this way it is also possible to avoid an iron mark which could spoil a good print.

• Check the fabric as some synthetics scorch easily and it may take time to discover just how hot you can get the iron before it causes the fabric to shrink and wrinkle and yet be hot enough to cause the chemical reaction necessary for a successful print. It is sometimes a good idea to use a piece of baking parchment over the top to diffuse the heat and to avoid scorching the fabric around the edge of the print.

• Make sure that the transfer paints are absolutely DRY before ironing off and if impatient dry them with a hair drier.

• Apply a really strong pressure and iron for long enough to ensure a good print. It is often the case that people stop too soon. Make sure that the whole print has been ironed sufficiently. Hold the paper firmly in place to prevent smudging the print, and peep underneath systematically working around the whole area. While holding the paper during the ironing process use a small pad of soft fabric to protect your hands from the extremely hot paper.

• At this point it might be wise to say that although transfer paints are very useful they are not ideal if you want an evenly repeated motif over a large area. In this case direct printing onto the fabric with another printing medium would be best.

• If after following all these guidelines the print is still weak or unsatisfactory then the fabric may well be the problem. It is sometimes difficult to tell the difference between a cotton and a polycotton and the results on a cotton will be more muted and not so colour fast.

• Having achieved some successfully transferred fabrics it can become compulsive to see how many different effects can be made on any available and suitable fabric. It is also a challenge to see how different prints can be obtained from a single piece of transferred paper until all the paint is used up and 'spent'. Do not discard the paper as it can be useful for collage and design work. You may wish to make a mark on the papers to avoid wasting time and energy in trying to iron off a spent print.

• Complex imagery with a build up of two or more prints on top of each other offers terrific opportunities for design ideas and in this book you will see some examples of the use of multi-layered prints.

• Fading in and out of focus images may be achieved by printing, then moving the print from one place to another. Real sensitivity will ensure that the iron is not so heavy at the edge that a hard line is formed. In this way colour and images can be delicately moved over the surface of a cloth.

• Take care not to allow frayed edges or strands of thread to spoil the print unless it is intended.

• Cutting the shape from the main paper makes it easier to register it back in place if any part needs re-ironing. This would be suitable if a clearly defined print is required.

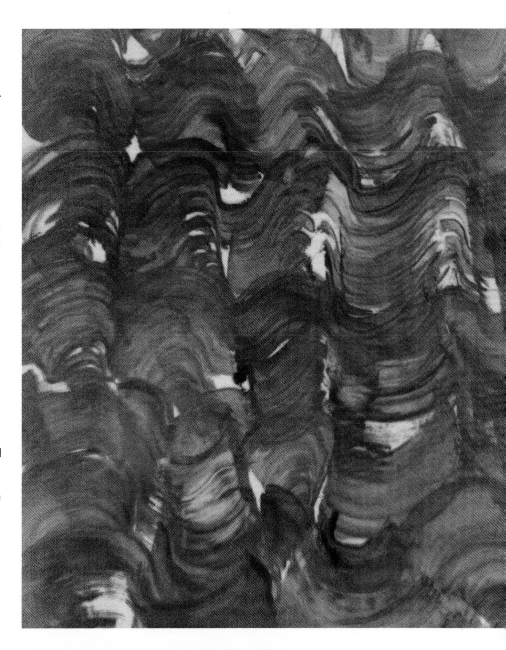

Above: *A card offcut dipped into several colours was used to create this wavy pattern printed on polyester lining material. J.B.*

Opposite: *Broad brush strokes created this sample printed on polyester cotton and illustrates how the cotton element in the cloth slightly softens the strong colour. J.B.*

Left: *'Busy Lizzie' flowers were dipped in paint and overprinted. Silk paint was flooded in afterwards. J.B.*

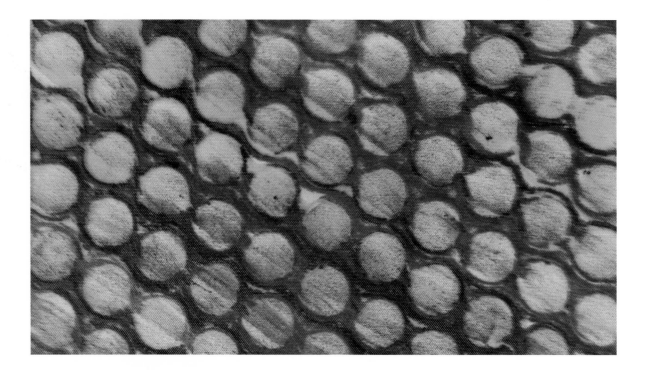

The comforting aspect to this technique is that the printing on fabric need not take place until you are reasonably happy with the image created on the paper.

A design or picture can be drawn or traced with a pencil onto the paper (remembering to reverse the image, see page 2) and then painted in the desired way. If you are not happy with the look after the first ironing reapply other colours.

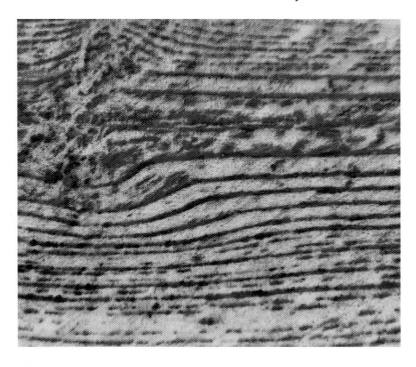

As well as exploiting within your design the individual characteristics of this medium it can be used just for transferring a coloured image to the fabric for covering with stitch. Canvas or machine stitches could be selected. It will be like a kit design with the very important difference in as much as it will be your own creation.

TRANSFER FABRIC CRAYONS are fun and so easy to use. Take time

to 'play' with them in order to discover the range of colours you can achieve. Patterns and pictures can be drawn and coloured in as well as being ideal for making rubbings. Intriguing textures to be found around your house or garden could provide the basis for your work or be integrated into your piece.

• Select a thinnish paper; photocopying or layout paper will be ideal. Place over the chosen area and crayon carefully but firmly over the surface. Experiment with several colours one over another to make colour variations.

• Sometimes the dark colours such as blue, violet and black can overpower a paler scheme as the last coloured crayon prints the strongest. Remember to use the darker ones first and top with the pinks, oranges and yellows.

• Initially applying a colour wash to the paper with transfer paints offers an alternative procedure. When the paper is dry take your rubbings with the transfer crayons. This action can be reversed by applying a thin paint wash afterwards. There is a slight colour change but the end result can appear more integrated.

Left: *An iron garden table and a section of fence provided two very different surfaces to make rubbings. The darker fabric transfer crayons were used first followed by the paler and brighter ones. J.B.*

Right: *Two landscapes, the same image but in different colour ways. The top shows a paler scheme with masking fluid grass textures resisting the paint, see page 8. The lower piece is in stronger tones. Both could be developed further with hand or machine stitches. The edging could suggest patterned couching or other decorative treatments.*
Lime, grey and olive greens could be made by mixing lemon yellow with small amounts of black. To make more of a khaki green add a trace of red. J.B.

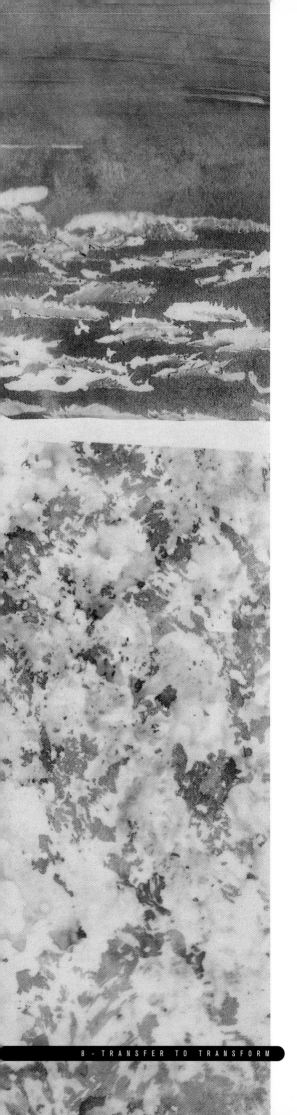

Resists

A resist is something which prevents dye or paint from penetrating an area of the surface. With transfer paints resists can be most effective in producing patterned and atmospheric designs.

Art masking fluid or drawing gum when painted or printed on paper resists any water based paints or inks to be applied. Generally used by watercolour or graphic artists, is is also an extremely useful method of resist to use with transfer fabric paints. It can have characteristics not dissimilar to batik.

Intricate designs drawn with a pencil on the paper can be re-traced with the fluid applied with a fine brush. Alternatively wonderful textural marks can be printed using the many items suggested in the printing section (see page 12.). Screwed up paper, card offcuts, printing blocks or plant matter could all be suitable. Allow time to practise in order to build up a 'dictionary' of textural marks which could suggest ideas for a number of interpretations such as water, spray, frothy flowers (eg. cow parsley), organic or architectural detailing.

Having applied the fluid or gum, wait for it to dry before applying the transfer paint. Test by gently touching the surface with your finger. If dry, none will transfer but it will feel slightly tacky.

Apply partially diluted paint gently over the surface. A brush or sponge applicator which has picked up several colours can result in surprising colour combinations. After a few seconds the masking fluid resists the paint and the patterns will re-emerge. Leave to dry before making the next creative decision which is whether or not to remove the fluid. Depending on the required image, it may be necessary to rub or peel away the masking gum. A putty rubber may help in this process. This will give a strong contrasting print. If a softer look is more appropriate leave the fluid in place. Although it in the main resists the paint when it is applied, a fine skim of colour is left on the surface so when it is printed on the material the image appears slightly less defined. Occasionally after ironing, traces of the fluid may be transferred to the fabric, this can be gently rubbed away.

• It can be extremely tedious removing dried fluid from brushes. Before using them and to avoid spoiling them immerse in water before working in plenty of soap. Wipe away the excess leaving the soap deep down within the 'roots'.

Left: These delicate greys and greens printed over masking fluid resist could suggest water spray or delicate flowers. J.B.

Right: The workbook samples shown here include crisply drawn patterns, textural marks made with card, sponge and an old brush. The letters were printed using a typesetters block. These letters read the same in reverse but do remember to trace through layout paper to reverse the letters that do not comply (see page 2). J.B.

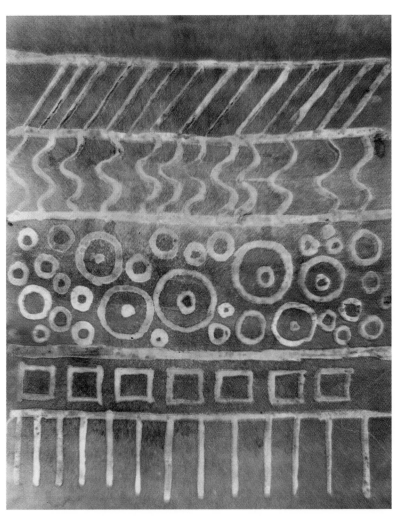

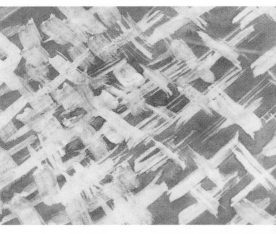
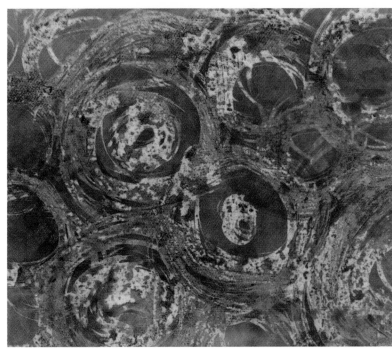

Sometimes people get an unwanted resist when they fail to check that there are loose fibres, threads or flecks of dust on the surface of the fabric. On lifting up the paper after ironing a quite dramatic voided shape can occur in a really difficult place.

There is a range of resists from natural plant materials, fibres and fabrics through to cut and torn paper.

To carry out this very simple but effective technique apply textured marks in various ways to papers and allow them to dry then try a variety of resists to find different ways of using this versatile technique. Feathers can be delicate and dramatic and skeletal leaves really repay the effort in ironing over them carefully. Fresh leaves and flowers also make effective resists but the sap or petals could stain the fabric. Cut paper patterns can be very intricate and if care is taken with the cutting the positive and negative shapes can be used to good effect.

A bonus of this technique is that it offers a secondary print in most cases. This is achieved by placing the leaf etc. in the usual way on the ground before ironing over a transfer paper. Pick up the leaf and turn it over then place it carefully on a new area of the ground. Place a piece of plain paper or silicone parchment over the leaf and iron firmly. In the first instance there will be a delicate print which happens because the fabric painted surface was absorbed by the leaf in the first ironing. In this way a number of resists including paper may be used.

Disappointingly, even though a variety of synthetic laces make good resists, they rarely offer a secondary print as the paper dyes them at the same time. However the coloured laces are subsequently excellent for free applique and textural effects.

Discharge using Transfer Paints.

There are times when a discharge (colour removal) effect may be needed and transfer paints offer this possibility. Firstly apply paint to a background paper as usual. A thick bleach used in a plastic dispenser with a nozzle can be drawn onto the paper where it will eat away at the colour. If the bleach is applied to wet paper it will bleed more than if applied dry. As always great care must be taken when handling bleach and it is best worked either outside or in a well ventilated room and wearing a mask. As the bleach dries the discharged pattern emerges. When fully dry the paper may be ironed off but there are fumes so it should be done either outside or using a mask for protection.

Left: Overlapping Petals

This technique gives at least two possible variations.

1. Starting from the top dried hydrangea petals were laid onto a polyester fabric and a sheet of heavily coloured transfer paper ironed over. Care should be taken not to move the leaves during the ironing process.

2. The petals resisted the transfer paint and became coloured in the process so the next stage was to pick them up, turn them over and place them carefully on the fabric and in this case in such a way as to blend the two images where they join. Before ironing they were covered with a piece of silicone baking sheet as extra protection.

With this method it is possible to achieve atmospheric in and out of focus images. A further variation is to actually paint the petals with transfer paints and this will result in stronger overprints. J.L.

Right: Velvet Piece

This richly patterned synthetic velvet started with a vivid turquoise colour which shines through the various patterns and textures which have been applied. The main element of the design is a fern which has been placed on the fabric and transfer painted paper ironed over once then moved and ironed several times. The leaf was also turned over and prints made from the reverse print method. The overprinting and shades of colouring have been blended and integrated by careful ironing. Finally some liquid gold surface paint was applied to the surface. J.L.

Printing

Printing in any of its numerous variations has great potential with transfer paints. In order to achieve good prints there are some considerations which will help.

• A thicker consistency of transfer paint will result in firmer prints so either use the ready mixed paints undiluted or mix a thickener with the powdered disperse dyes.

• Make sure that the printing surface is suitable for good prints, particularly when using wooden blocks or potato prints where a hard surface may not achieve the best contact. Of all the surfaces tried the metalised ironing board cloth with a fine foam backing is the nearest to a professional printing surface that we can find.

• It may be better to apply the paint to the printing block with a paintbrush rather than dip it into paint. It will achieve a good coating and avoid waste and it is also possible to apply more than one colour on the motif to gain interesting effects.

• **The one, two, three method.** When printing with plant materials, feathers etc. have a good supply of paper available. Place the feather on a piece of paper and apply the transfer paint with a sponge etc. in such a way that any excess will be caught by the backing paper and with care form a good negative shape. When the feather has been well covered in paint place it paint side down on a second piece of paper and place a third over the top to rub the print firmly with fingers or a roller to achieve a really good impression and on lifting this paper not only will you have a good print but the rubbing paper often has 'ghosted shapes' which will also print off thus giving three for the price of one. When ironing off, the three images may be overlapped and interspersed with each other for atmospheric imagery.

• As well as printing blocks, hand made or bought, there are stencils and templates, doilies', plastic lace etc. Just picking up things to hand such as pencil ends, rubbers, pieces of card, cotton wool buds even fingers work well, very little is sacred.

• There is a real excitement in interiors at present and although it is perfectly possible to cut your own stencils and printing blocks there are some useful professionally made ones which will save time and prove to be effective if used with discretion and these include checkerboard effect, stripes and simple geometric motifs which are widely available at craft centres, art and hardware shops.

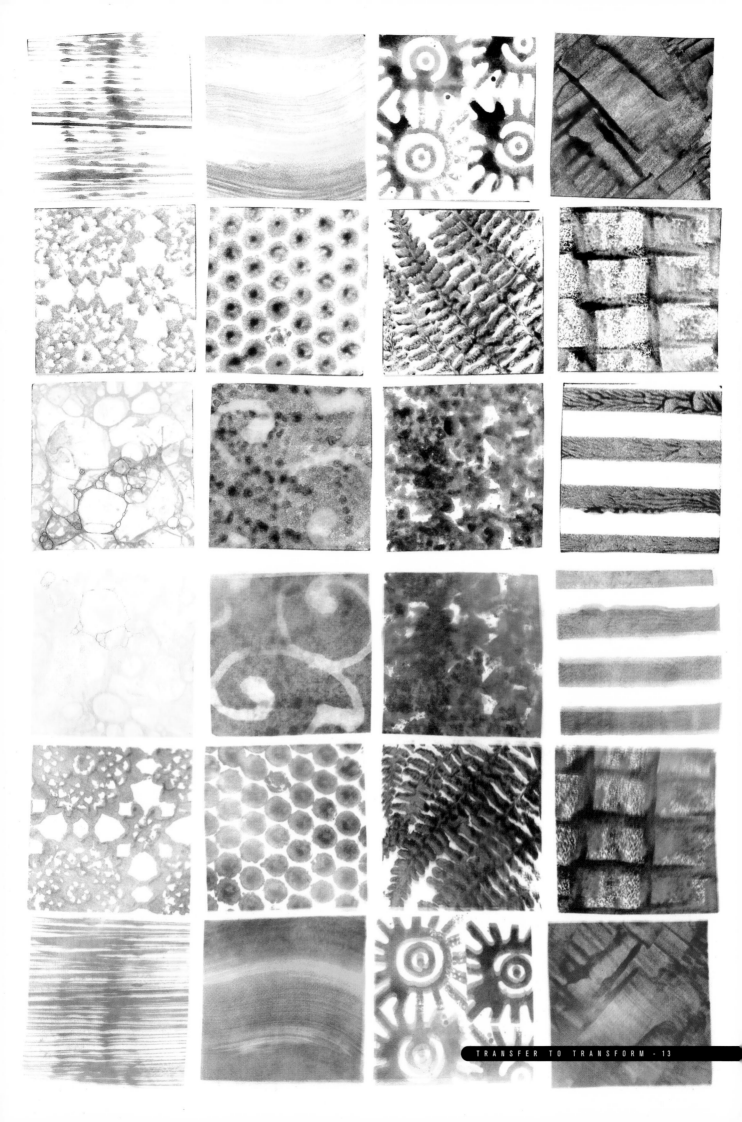

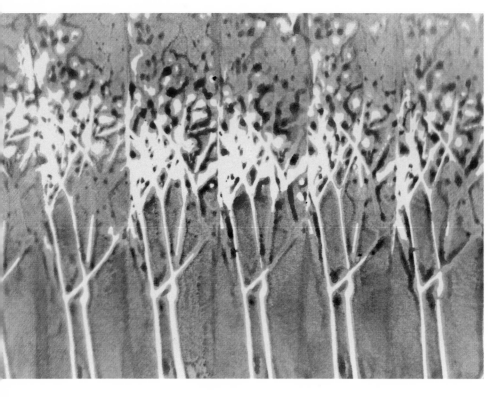

Right: *A wooden block printed onto polyester cotton formed a simple but effective decoration. Similar prints on a sheer synthetic was placed on top to partially diffuse the pattern. Straight stitches in fine wool and silk threads emphasise some of the rhythms. J.B.*

Left & Below: *The new printing foam was used for this series of experiments. Gypsophila flowers, a daisy and a 'dog' broach were the motifs used. The paint was applied by sponge or dipped into the paint palette. J.B.*

Making your own printing blocks may be challenging. Patterns cut out from a block of foam with scissors or a craft knife offer an interesting but less hard edged result.

However there are other materials now available for us to experiment with. Becoming easier to track down is a type of foam which is magical and such a useful addition to your design equipment. In order to make a printing block, the smoother surface needs to be heated. We suggest covering it with baking parchment for protection and gently ironing the surface for a few seconds. While it is still warm it can be placed and pressed down over items such as plant forms, jewellery and other textural surfaces. To achieve a good impression you may need to press firmly and slightly 'rock' the foam to indent clearly. Roll,

brush, sponge or stamp the block with transfer paint and print on paper in the normal way. If you are not satisfied with the image or you have completed the printing, gently warm the surface as before and it will revert to its original state ready for the next imprint! Gluing the foam to a wood block may make it easier to handle.

• It is sold in packs of pre-cut shapes or in sheet form where you can determine and cut the size of the block you need.

• The image does not print as cleanly cut and detailed as the imprint suggests but gives a freer textural result.

• As with all printing, dipping the brush or sponge into several colours or not cleaning out the previous colour too well often results in unexpected and pleasing colour schemes.

Many of these suggestions can be combined to create unique surfaces to develop further.

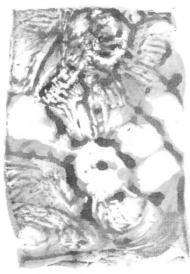

Mono-Printing

Monoprinting is the process whereby figurative or abstract patterns are drawn into a layer of printing ink or paint (including fabric paint) which has been rolled onto a smooth surface such as glass or plastic. A print is taken by gently pressing paper over the image. Unexpected and exciting prints can be created by using transfer fabric paints in this way. It is a quick and simple method which can produce sensitively textured imagery or boldly vibrant passages of colour. This type of printing exploits its own unique characteristics without effecting the feel of the cloth.

Always allow lots of time to experiment. Try various colour combinations and learn to judge the right amounts of paint to use as well as ways of imprinting and drawing into the paint. Keep a notebook for samples.

To experience this method, you will need a medium sized sheet of thick glass A3 (420x297mm). For protection, the edges should be professionally 'ground' or covered with strong tape. Other non-porous materials such as formica, perspex or industrial polythene sheeting can be used and will produce different effects. Use a transfer paint which has a thicker consistency. Other paints which are too fluid will not be suitable unless a thickening medium is added. As with all printing cover the work surfaces.

• Dribble several coloured transfer paints onto the glass. Using a roller, lightly spread the paint over the glass partially mixing the colour and developing textural patterns. Do not over mix the paint as it could end up looking like mud. Spreading the paint with a broad brush or sponge applicator gives an alternative effect.

• Place a sheet of paper on the glass and press down using the side of your hand or a clean roller. Gently smooth over the whole area.

• Peel the paper away and leave to dry. Glass prints can produce exciting effects in their own right.

• Wipe the surface clean with a dampened cloth. Dry carefully with kitchen paper towel before continuing with the application of more paint.

Intriguing prints can result from drawing patterns into the paint. Card offcuts, sticks and other implements can be used to draw or write into the wet surface. Finely pointed tools are not so effective as unlike traditional printing ink the medium is not stable enough to hold the line. Speed is the essence as the water based paint dries quickly.

Flowers, leaves, wood or foam blocks can be pressed onto the surface lifting some of the paint away and leaving behind subtle, understated imprints. Remember not to apply the paint too thickly as it will smudge and not hold the drawn image as successfully as a skim of paint rolled over the glass.

One important factor to note is unlike normal transfer painting where a pattern or picture is reversed on printing, this is not the case with this method. A word incised in the paint will show in reverse on the paper print but will revert the right way when it is transferred from the paper to the cloth. With experience you will be able to anticipate certain results but with this method of printing there will always be an element of surprise which in its self can lead you down other avenues of thought offering new challenges and the development of design ideas.

Top: *This monoprint was created by rolling the paint in strong movements over the glass before pressing flower heads into the paint. This could easily form the basis for further development of flowers and undergrowth. Notice the unexpected and subtle colours within the whole piece. J.B.*

Left: *This word was drawn into the wet fabric paint using a wooden stick with a chiselled end which gives an italic flourish. Remember that in this method the word can be drawn to read the right way and will revert again once the paper is printed onto the fabric. J.B.*

Right: *Vibrant colours were rolled onto the glass. Roller textures and slightly crumpled paper add further textures. Printed on polyester lining material. J.B.*

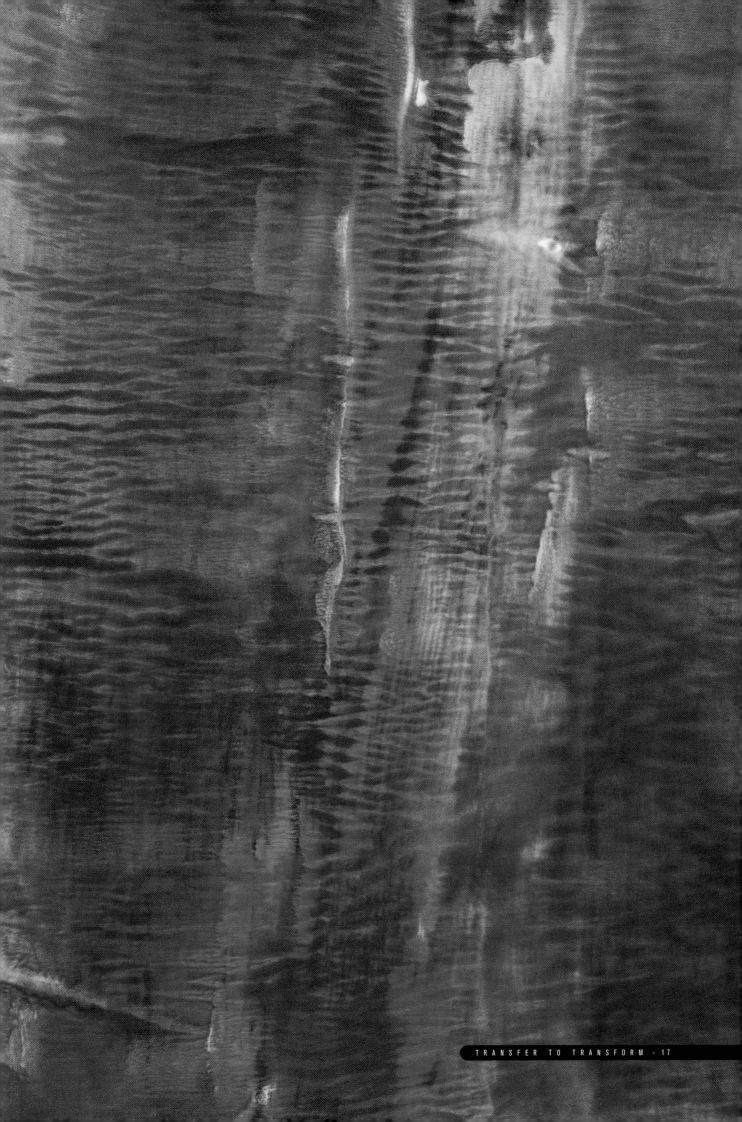

Layering

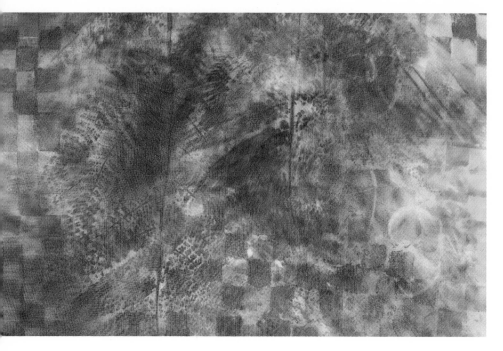

Perhaps the most exciting and mysterious effects are to be gained by mixing prints and building up. Here is where the use of transfer paints has amazing advantages over other techniques.

Imagine depicting several different aspects of a subject and incorporating them in one image. Although there are many ways of doing this the use of transfer paints offers great potential. If each of the different elements is painted or printed onto a different piece of paper and they are then used together and overprinted, the combinations of imagery may well capture the essence of the subject almost effortlessly.

This would be an excellent way of representing a visit to Paris for example. The cathedrals and architecture could feature as one element and the wonderful pots of highly coloured geraniums as another. When combined they will be abstracted and yet give the impression of the city in a more significant way than either on its own.

There are a few points which need to be thought about if this technique is to succeed.

• It is usually best to work from lighter to darker colours.

• The prints may be cut or torn to isolate required elements before ironing off.

• Think about an underpinning composition to hold the diverse elements together.

• To eliminate white or obvious backgrounds iron off a fine wash of colour first.

If there are several different images to be used consider which one will be the major focus so that it can be given some emphasis and help co-ordinate the composition.

Combining, Building & Cutting Back

Having ironed off a selection of prints on a wide range of fabrics you will now have a series of potential backgrounds and the next stage can be problematic. Some will be so beautiful that you won't want to do anything to them at all but most of us want to achieve seductive or compelling imagery for hand and/or machine stitching and there are strategies which may be employed to used them to good effect.

Cutting the print in different ways and applying it to a ground in a variety of configurations offers enormous potential. The ground fabric could be plain or transfer painted and in a contrasting colour and texture or in harmony with the print. There is excellent potential here for mixing thick and thin fabrics in unexpected and dynamic juxtapositions. The simplest way to achieve this is by ironing the print onto 'Bondaweb' to make the cutting easier to handle. Place the shapes into position before removing the paper backing and ironing into place. Stitching may be added to enhance the image and to secure the pieces onto the background.

Different qualities of fabric layered on top of each other and stitched in various ways before cutting back produces richly textured surfaces. Thick velvety fabrics can protrude through fine and delicate layers in unusual combinations.

Different coloured lamés which have been transfer painted retain their sheen but lose their brashness and look subtle but dynamic under sheer fabrics. Canvas can contrast with lace or synthetic velvet.

Since these materials all contain synthetic fibres they will also respond to heat and will burn with varying degrees of success. Always make sure that you work in a well ventilated area, outside or wear a mask. Soldering irons or stencil cutters with the finest points may be used to cut through layers and inscribe designs. The edges of the fabric will also be sealed limiting the fraying process. They can alter the surface of the synthetic fibres to produce a less obvious texture.

It may be the fact that transfer fabrics require synthetic fabrics for their success which prevents people from using them as many find them unsympathetic. With the various methods described we can change the colour and the quality of surface to make them more useful.

Left: Cushions

Lovely fabrics are produced with transfer. These cushions demonstrate how easy it is to work with these colourful fabrics in a simple but effective way. The printed synthetic velvets were ironed onto 'Bondaweb' before being cut up and applied to a simple linen ground. They also demonstrate that understated and subtle colour combinations are possible. The shapes have been machined to make them hard wearing and the most delicate shaded threads with automatic patterns finishes the spaces between the shapes. J.L.

Right: Tree bark (notebook page)

This textured piece based on a tree bark has three layers each of which has been printed with a transfer painted image. Although this may at first seem wasteful the sensitive colour ways do add an extra dimension. The top layer is sheer cheap curtain netting and a coloured gold lame adds the crusty sparkle to a base of synthetic velvet. These layers have been stitched together and cut back before using a fine soldering tool to draw in some detailing and reveal the three layers. Hand stitching followed by machine embroidery completes the surface texture. The colours which are possible with transfer paints are exciting and subtle so care needs to be taken in selecting sympathetic threads. J.L.

Far Right: Tree bark print (notebook page)

This print which inspired the piece was made with a slightly dampened sponge which was printed taking care to apply more pressure on the darker side to give the illusion of roundness. The lighter marks were made by discharging the colour with thick bleach in a dispenser (be sure to iron this off outside or using a mask). J.L.

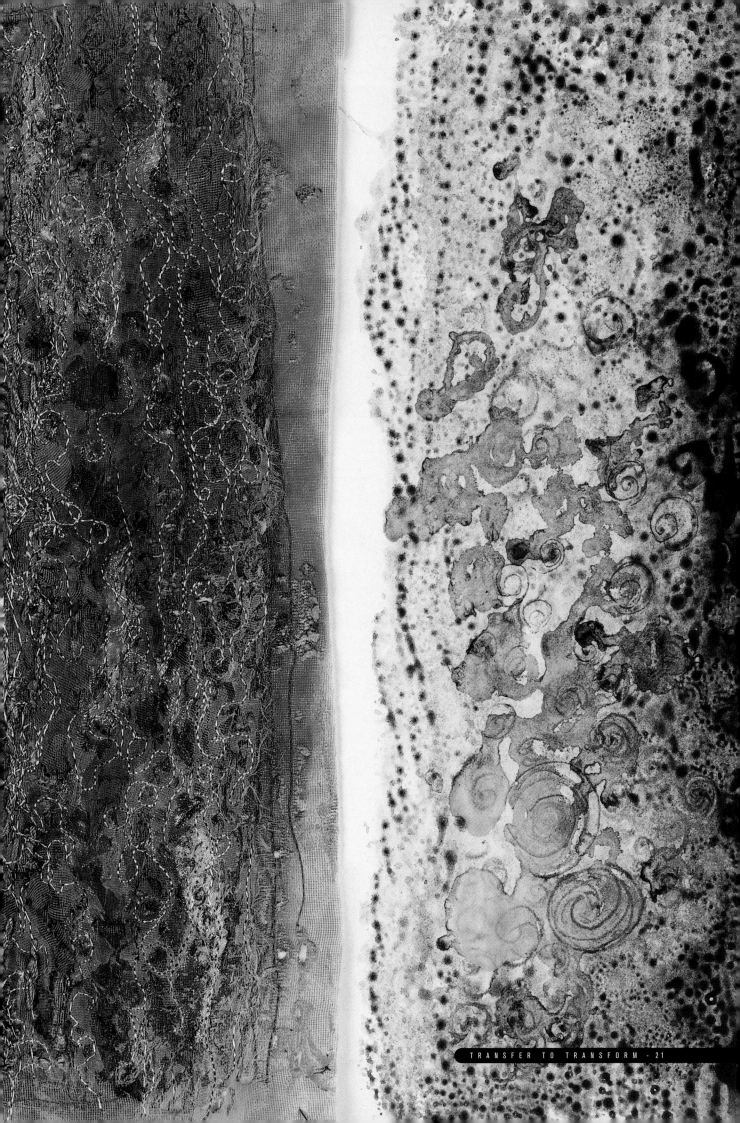

Stitching

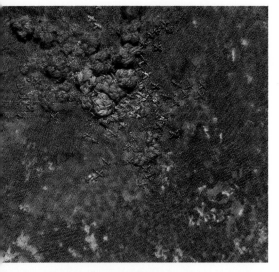

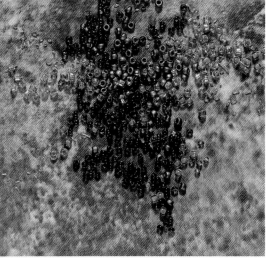

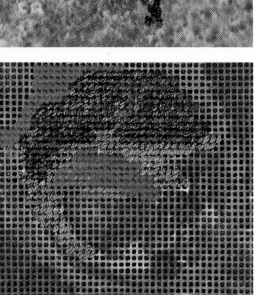

As you can see the versatility of transfer fabric paints and crayons is far reaching. Patterned or atmospheric imagery can provide the starting point or base for a range of interpretations such as undergrowth, gardens, old walls, rock faces, sky or seascapes and all manner of decorative effects. Additional applique, hand and machine stitches, can be integrated to form a successful textile. Do always consider the following points.

• As ever, one of the secrets of stitching is to be totally sensitive to the background fabric so that the stitching emerges from the cloth.

• With the printed fabrics it may not be necessary to overwhelm them with stitch but to add a further dimension of surface and enrich the patterning.

• Sometimes the prints will develop into wonderful images and the stitching will completely cover them up. Then they will have served their purpose as an inspiration.

• The selection of threads will be important particularly with respect to tonal values as the colours produced on the backgrounds may be subtle and difficult to match.

• The weight, quality and texture of the threads should be in keeping with the background.

• The selection of the stitch should reflect the subject matter. Simple stitches such as straight, seeding and free cross often work well and blend with the printed grounds.

• If extensive stitching is to be carried out on a fine fabric it may need to be supported on a firm fabric first.

Top Left: *This richly coloured sponged pattern offers much scope for adding textural stitches such as sorbello, cross and seeding to develop the fabric. Care needs to be taken to select colours that blend and 'grow' out of the background. J.B.*

Middle Left: *These samples illustrate how subtle colour schemes can inspire colour and textural choices. The simple sponged texture has been emphasised with tiny beads and this type of approach could be developed further and used in surface decoration for fashion or accessories. J.B.*

Bottom Left: *Transfer fabric printing is a fabulous way of transferring your coloured design to canvas. Here are a few tent stitches which have been worked to illustrate this point. J.B.*

Right: *This delicately coloured embroidery shows the layering of simple daisy prints. The base cloth is a blue metallic, the top is an extremely sheer fabric. Machine stitches have traced the shapes in an informal way. Further highlighting is worked in silk running or cross stitches. J.B.*

Trouble Shooting

Despite years of experience with using transfer paints there are still times when things don't go to plan so a check list is often a good idea. Sometimes the mistakes have resulted in the most exciting work.

• If the prints are unsuccessful then don't forget to check that you have been using transfer paints as at least one manufacturer uses a similar bottle for different types of dye.

• Paper may be too soft. Use one that is more polished and non-absorbent.

• Check the heat of the iron and if possible check with another iron to see if your iron reaches a sufficient heat for the process.

• Make sure that the iron has not been switched off as electricity is fundamental to the process!

• Check that the fabric is a synthetic mix and not a natural fibre such as cotton.

• If a print is patchy it may be possible to overprint in selected areas to blend in a colour. With very delicate areas just use the point of the iron.

• Unlike ironing shirts or sheets, take time to iron slowly for longer and with sustained pressure. Take care not to move the paper unless a blurred out of focus image is required.

• Remember that in many cases the transfer print is only the first stage of making an individual textile and that appliqué, hand, and machine embroidery can contribute to the creation of a wholly considered piece.

Armed with the techniques described in this book and the range of possibilities explored we know that we have still only touched the surface of this hugely rewarding area. We fully intend to exploit these ideas further and hope that transfer paints may undergo a revival once their true potential has been realised.

Suppliers

Art Van Go
16 Hollybush Lane, Datchworth, Knebworth, Herts, SG3 6RE
Tel. 01438 814946
Fabric paints, printing foams, drawing gum, general supplies.

Kerntex Services Ltd
Chorley Business & Technology Centre, Euxton Lane, Chorley, Lancashire PR7 6TE. Tel. 01257 230220
Comprehensive range of dyes and fabric paints.

Gillsew
Boundary House, Moor Common, Lane End, Bucks HP14 3HR.
Tel. 12494 881886
General embroidery supplies, printing blocks, soft scuplt, fabric paints.

George Weill Mail Order.
20 Reading Arch Road, Redhill, Surrey, RH1 1H6
Tel. 01737 778868
Fabric paints/dye.

Left: Spent papers used for collage. J.L.

Inside back cover: Cut paper resists formed the basic pattern for this diffused old tile image. By moving the template around and overprinting with positive and negative shapes the in and out of focus image was achieved. J.L.

Inca Studio Ltd. - 10 Duke Street, Princes Risborough, Bucks, HP27 0AT.
Tel. 01844 343343 - Fabric paints, general embroidery supplies.

Sax Arts & Crafts
PO Box 510710.New Berlin.
Wi. 53151-0710. USA
Tel. 001 800 558 6696
Pre cut shapes or sheets, 'pen score' foam.

Quilters' Resource Inc.
Double Trouble & Textile publications,USA. PO BOX 148850, Chicago, IL60614. Tel. 773 278 5695

A comprehensive list of suppliers can be found in the Small Ads section of

The World of Embroidery published by the Embroiderers' Guild. Apt. 41 Hampton Court Palace, East Molesey, Surrey, KT8 9BB
Tel. 0181 943 1229

Further Reading

Vanishing Act, Bk-1 - Jan Beaney. Double Trouble Enterprises.

Voluptuous Velvet, Bk-2
- Jean Littlejohn.
Double Trouble Enterprises.

Bonding and Beyond, Bk-3
- Jan Beaney & Jean Littlejohn. Double Trouble Enterprises.

The Art of the Needle -
Jan Beaney. Century.

A Complete Guide to Creative Embroidery - Jan Beaney & Jean Littlejohn. Batsford Books.

Stitch Magic – Jan Beaney & Jean Littlejohn. Batsford Books.

Fabric Painting for Embroidery – Valerie Campbell Harding. Batsford Books.

Imagery on Fabric –
Jean Ray Laury. A complete surface design handbook.
ISBN 1-57120-034. C & T Publishing, Inc. PO Box 1456. Lafayette, CA 94549. USA

Acknowledgements

Many, many thanks as ever go to our husbands Steve and Philip for their continued support, to Jan's daughter Victoria for her patience and typing skills, to Michael Wicks for his super photography and last but not least to Jason Horsburgh for sympathetically taking our ideas on board and creating an attractive layout.